D1530299

The Big Golden Book of Fairy Tales

Retold by
LORNIE LEETE-HODGE
Illustrated by
BEVERLIE MANSON

GOLDEN PRESS • NEW YORK
Western Publishing Company, Inc., Racine, Wisconsin

Copyright © 1981, 1978 by The Hamlyn Publishing Group Limited. All rights reserved. Printed in Singapore. No part of this publication may be reproduced, in any form, without the permission of The Hamlyn Publishing Group Limited. Published in the U.S.A. by Western Publishing Company, Inc. GOLDEN®, A GOLDEN BOOK®, and GOLDEN PRESS® are trademarks of Western Publishing Company, Inc. Library of Congress Catalog Card Number: 82-80891   ISBN 0-307-95545-1   A B C D E F G H I J

Contents

The Emperor's New Clothes

Many years ago there lived an Emperor who was fat and proud and very vain. All he cared for was new clothes. He did not trouble himself about his country, his army or his people – all he wanted to do was to show off his fine clothes. No one has ever had so many clothes, for this emperor had a suit for every hour of the day. If anyone wanted to see him, his ministers did not say, as they would with other emperors, 'He is in the Council Chamber.' They would always reply, 'He is in his wardrobe.'

Life was very gay in the great city where he lived. One day two strangers arrived. They were rogues who called themselves weavers, and they told everyone that they knew how to weave the most beautiful patterns in the world, and make the most beautiful material ever seen. In fact, they said, their clothes were magic, and were invisible to everyone who was unfit for his high office, or who was just stupid.

'Good gracious me!' said everyone who heard this. 'What wonderful cloth!'

Of course, as the weavers intended, the Emperor heard about the magic cloth and sent for them to make him more suits.

'If I wear such clothes, I could find out which men in my kingdom are unfit for the offices they hold. I could tell wise men from fools. I must have this cloth this very day!'

So the Emperor gave the two weavers a lot of money and told them to make him the finest suits in the world. The two rogues set up their looms and pretended to be very busy indeed, demanding the very best silk and gold thread, which they put into their bags, and they worked far into the night on the empty looms in the palace.

'I wonder how they are getting on?' thought the Emperor, and then he remembered that a fool or someone unfit for office could not see the fine cloth. 'I must not risk it myself,' he said. 'I will send my Prime Minister to find out for me.'

So the Prime Minister went into the great hall where the weavers were working with all their might on the empty looms.

'What is the meaning of this?' thought the old man, rubbing his eyes. 'I cannot see a single strand of thread on the looms!' But he did not say anything.

The weavers watched him. 'What do you think?' they asked him. 'Will the Emperor be pleased?'

The Prime Minister knew he must say something or appear a fool, so he clapped his hands and said, 'Oh, it is quite lovely! The Emperor will be delighted.'

The weavers told him the texture and the pattern and he pretended to feel the material in his hands, and exclaimed at the beautiful colours. He listened very hard to all they said and went back to the Emperor and repeated it to him.

The Emperor was getting impatient. So he sent another minister to the weavers to ask about his new clothes. He too went to the looms and saw nothing, but he listened carefully to the weavers and then told the Emperor how wonderful the suits would be.

12

Soon the whole city was talking of the wonderful material the Emperor had ordered and how magnificent he would look in his new finery.

At last the Emperor could wait no longer. He had to see for himself. Of course he could see nothing, but he pretended to admire the softness of the cloth, and the lavish, vivid colours. 'Wonderful, wonderful,' he said. 'It has my approval.' For he would not admit there was nothing to be seen, not with everyone watching.

The whole court looked on and wondered. No one saw anything, but all copied the Emperor in saying that the new clothes were magnificent, and he would look perfect wearing them.

'Why not show these fine clothes to the whole city?' the Prime Minister suggested. 'We could have a procession, and everyone would see the Emperor in his finest suit.'

They all clapped their hands and said it was a wonderful idea.

At last the great day dawned. The previous night the two weavers had been with their looms until dawn, and said the suit was perfection itself. As the Emperor and his whole court stood and watched, the weavers held up their arms, just as if they actually were holding something. 'See,' they said, 'here are the breeches! Here is the coat! This is the cloak! Feel the smoothness, see the richness of the colour.'

'These clothes are so fine,' the weavers continued, 'so comfortable that you will believe you have nothing on at all! That is the secret of the magic.'

'Will Your Majesty please take off your clothes, and we can help you to put on your new clothes. See here, in this mirror, and you will be astonished.'

So the Emperor removed his clothes, and the weavers bowed low before him and held up their arms, pretending to help him, first into the silk shirt they had made, then the breeches, and so on, until at last they placed the cloak round his shoulders and said he was ready. All the while the Emperor turned this way and that, preening himself before the huge mirror.

The Master of Ceremonies announced that the great procession was ready. All the court had lined up behind the Emperor, who had now placed his crown upon his head. He stepped out into the roadway, and four courtiers held a grand canopy above his head, four more bent down as if to pick up his train and the procession was ready to move.

The streets were filled with a cheering crowd of people, and they had crowded to the windows all along the route of the procession.

'Doesn't he look fine? What a magnificent suit! The Emperor has never looked so magnificent!' cried the people as he passed, preening and smiling, down the busy streets.

No one would admit they could see nothing, for no one wanted to look a fool. Everyone clapped his hands and praised the Emperor's new clothes.

Everyone, that is, except one small boy who stood on the edge of the pavement. He was small and ragged with bare feet, and he looked in surprise at the Emperor coming towards him.

'But he has nothing on!' he cried loudly.

'Sssh, what are you saying?' said his father.

'But it's true,' said the boy. 'The Emperor has nothing on!'

All round, people heard the child and began to whisper it to each other. 'He has nothing on!' At last the whisper grew into a shout, and soon the whole city was shouting, 'HE HAS NOTHING ON!'

The Emperor felt very embarrassed, for he knew the people were right. But he knew he must not run away, so he drew himself up to his full height, squared his shoulders and walked on, even pretending to trip over the train that was not there.

Snow White and Rose Red

Once there was a poor widow who lived in a tiny little cottage, in front of which were two beautiful rose trees. One tree always bore white roses and on the other there were always red roses. The widow had two daughters who were just like the two trees. The girls' names were Snow White and Rose Red, and they were the sweetest and best children in the whole world!

Snow White was very fair, with blue eyes and long silky hair, while Rose Red had dark curly hair, sparkling brown eyes and rosy cheeks. The two girls loved each other very dearly and went everywhere together.

Rose Red loved to run about in the fields and meadows to pick flowers, and Snow White, who also liked to help her mother in the house, would take her hand and they would walk together in the woods and fields.

Though they roamed far from home in the wild forest gathering berries and flowers, no beast ever harmed them. Instead, the animals would come up to the sisters as if they knew that Snow White and Rose Red would be kind to them. The little brown hare, usually so timid, would eat from their hands, the deer grazed beside them and the birds would sit on the branches of the trees and sing to them. No evil ever befell them.

In the winter, the family would all stay together by the glow of

the warm fire. Sometimes, when they had finished their work, the sisters would stoke up the fire, light the candles and bring out their spindles while their mother read to them.

One evening, when the frost was very cold and the snow had fallen, the family were sitting comfortably by the fire. A small white dove which they had found in the snow nestled against Snow White, his tiny head tucked under his wing. A baby lamb, brought in from the hills, lay fast asleep by the hearth, his little hoofs shining in the glow of the firelight.

Suddenly there was a loud knock on the front door. 'Open the door, Rose Red,' said her mother. Rose Red jumped up and pulled back the bolts, thinking some traveller was lost in the snow.

Then she screamed! For instead of the traveller Rose Red expected to find on the doorstep, there stood a large, shaggy bear! The lamb began to bleat and the dove flew in circles high above the room. Snow White clasped her sister's hand and the girls ran to their mother.

'Don't be afraid,' said the bear. 'I won't hurt you. I am half frozen with the cold! May I warm myself a little?'

'Oh, you poor bear,' said Mother. 'Do come inside by the fire. Be careful not to singe your fur.'

The bear came in and sat by the fire and the little lamb bleated a welcome.

'Come along, Rose Red and Snow White,' said Mother, 'the bear won't hurt you. He is a good, honest creature.'

So the girls came up to the great, big bear who asked them to beat the snow from his coat. They fetched a brush and rubbed him until he was dry and fluffy. Then the great beast lay down in front of the glowing fire and growled contentedly. Rose Red and Snow White quite forgot their fears and began to play with him, as they would with a big dog. They rolled him here and there, and if he growled, they just laughed.

The bear enjoyed their game, but when they went too far in their excitement, he said softly,

'Oh spare my life!
Snow White and Rose Red
Will you beat your lover dead?'

At last Mother banked up the fire and sent the girls to bed. She put out her candle and said goodnight to the bear, telling him he could lie by the hearth until morning.

As soon as it was light the bear seemed in a hurry to go, so the girls waved him goodbye and watched him disappear into the forest, his paws making big prints in the crisp snow.

Every evening that winter at the same time, the bear came to the door, just as he had done the first night. The girls brushed his fur until it was dry and played games with him, and then he lay by the hearth until morning.

The family soon got so used to the bear that they never locked the door at night until their huge, furry friend had come in.

Spring came and the sun warmed the land once more, melting the white snow and the clear icicles. Everything in the forest grew green and one morning the bear said to Snow White, 'Now I must go away, and not come back until the summer is over!'

'Oh, do stay, dear bear,' said Snow White who was by now very fond of him. 'Where are you going?'

'I have to stay in the forest to guard my treasures,' he told her. 'Some dwarfs that you may meet in the forest are good, but others are mean and spiteful, and may be thieves as well!'

'Don't they steal in the winter?' asked Rose Red.

'No, they live underground where the land is rock hard. They go below before the earth freezes, to keep warm, and there they stay until the spring sun shines again. Then nothing is safe, for what the dwarfs take is never seen again.'

Snow White and Rose Red were very sad to see their friend leave them, but he seemed in a hurry to go. As they unbolted the door his fur caught in the latch and they were sure they had seen a glint of gold beneath his coat. But the bear did not turn round – he hurried off into the trees and was soon lost to sight.

During the cold winter the family had used up all their store of firewood so the girls went into the forest to collect more to fill up the woodshed. As they walked they picked up fallen branches and put them into their small cart, and they saw that a huge tree had fallen into the long grass. Something was jumping up and down beside it but they could not see what it was. At first they thought it might be a squirrel, but soon they found it was a little dwarf. He had such a long white beard, quite as long as himself, and a bad-tempered, shrivelled face. Snow White could see that his beard was caught in the tree, and he was jumping about like a dog on a chain. When he saw the girls he cried out, 'Don't just stand there! Come and help me!'

'Whatever happened, little man?' asked Rose Red.

'You silly goose!' shouted the dwarf. 'I was trying to split the tree to get chips for the fire, but the wood was slippery and the wedge fell out. It caught my beautiful, long beard. Don't you laugh at me, you silly milk-faced things. Just get me out!'

Snow White and Rose Red tried hard to free the dwarf, but he was caught fast in the tree.

'I will fetch help,' said Rose Red.

'No time for that!' snapped the dwarf. '*Do* something, you wretched girl!'

'Don't be so impatient,' said Snow White, 'I will help you. Hold still a minute.' She took her scissors from her pocket and snipped the end off his beard. As soon as he was free the dwarf snatched a bag of gold hidden among the roots of the tree, and went off, muttering to himself, 'Stupid girls! Fancy cutting my splendid beard.' And he was gone, without a word of thanks for their help.

23

A few days later Snow White and Rose Red went to the stream to catch a fish for supper. As they came near they could see the water was swirling and swishing about and they noticed something that looked like a huge grasshopper jumping up and down along the bank. They ran forward to see what this could possibly be and found it was the dwarf they had helped when he was caught in the tree.

'What are you doing?' asked Rose Red. 'Are you going to jump into the water? It's quite deep there, so do be careful.'

'Can't you see anything, you stupid girl?' cried the dwarf in a rage. 'This wretched fish is trying to pull me into the water!'

Tugging angrily at the part of his beard below the water, the dwarf explained that he had been sitting on the river bank fishing when a puff of wind had tangled his beard in the fishing line, just at the moment a big fish had taken the bait. The fish had pulled one way and the dwarf had pulled another. Back and forth they had pulled and tugged and now the fish was tiring the dwarf. He would soon be in the stream.

The girls saw how the dwarf clung to every blade of grass and every tall weed, yet could not save himself. So they held him firmly and tried to disentangle the beard from the hook and line, but it was too tightly caught. There was nothing else to do but cut the beard once more. Snow White made a quick snip with her scissors and the dwarf was free again.

'You wretched girl!' he screamed at poor Snow White. 'You have ruined my face! Look at the mess I am in. First you cut off the tip of my beard, and now quite half of it is gone. All the other dwarfs will laugh at me. Oh! Oh! Oh!' And he stamped his tiny feet in rage. Then the little figure bent and picked up a bag of pearls which had been hidden in the rushes. He put the bag on his back and stamped off without a word of thanks.

Not long after this the girls' mother sent them into town to
buy needles and laces and ribbons. The road led over a field
where large boulders lay scattered, and as they walked along they
saw a huge bird hovering in the air, circling slowly above them.
Then, descending very slowly, it landed on a rock not far away.
As soon as it dropped they heard a sharp, piercing cry and ran to
see what was happening.

To their horror they saw that the huge bird had seized the
dwarf in his talons and was going to make off with him. The
kind-hearted girls rushed up and took hold of the little dwarf,

26

struggling with all their strength against the huge bird which flapped its wings in an effort to beat them off. At last they managed to drive it away and the dwarf was free once more.

'Clumsy fools!' he berated them. 'Couldn't you have been more careful? Just look at my fine clothes! All torn and ruined. You stupid things!' And, picking up a bag of precious stones, he vanished under the rocks and into his cave.

The girls laughed, paying no attention to his rudeness, and went on their journey into the town. On the way home they passed through the field again and were very surprised to see the dwarf setting out his precious stones on an open piece of ground. He had thought no one would pass in the late afternoon. The setting sun shone on the glittering stones, making them sparkle and dance so beautifully that the two girls stopped to look.

'What are you gaping at?' shrieked the dwarf crossly, his face scarlet with rage. 'Be off with you!' And he shook his tiny fist at them.

Just then there was a low growl and a huge bear lumbered out of the wood. The dwarf jumped up in terror, but he had no time to hide for the bear was upon him.

'Mister Bear!' he screamed. 'Spare me! I'll give you all my treasure. Look at these beautiful stones on the ground. Spare me! Seize these wicked girls, they will make a better meal for you. Spare me!'

The bear stood quite still while the dwarf was speaking then he gave another deep growl, reared up on his hind legs, and knocked the dwarf on the head. The bad-tempered little creature never moved again.

Terrified, the girls ran away, but the bear called after them. 'Snow White! Rose Red! Wait! Do not be afraid, I will not hurt you.' They turned and saw it was the bear they knew and they ran to meet him with joyous cries. Suddenly, his bearskin fell to the ground and before them stood a handsome young man, dressed in bright gold.

'I am a king's son,' he told them, 'and I was bewitched by that wicked dwarf. He stole my treasure and I was doomed to roam about the woods as a wild bear until his death should set me free. Now at last the spell is broken and I am free. But I should have perished without your kindness in the cold winter.'

Soon, all three set off to the cottage to tell the girls' mother what had happened. The prince had to return to his father, but he promised to return to see them.

Next time he came he brought his younger brother with him, and he was just as handsome! The prince asked Snow White to marry him, and his brother asked for Rose Red's hand in marriage.

The happy couples went back to live in the king's palace, taking the dwarf's treasure with them. The girls' mother came too, of course, and she brought her beautiful rose trees with her. They stood in front of her window, and blossomed every year – one tree a beautiful red, the other as white as snow.

Hansel and Gretel

Close to the edge of a great forest there lived a poor woodcutter with his wife and children. There was a boy, Hansel, and a girl, Gretel. The family were very poor and often there was not enough food for them all to eat.

One night the woodcutter said to his wife, 'What can we do? There is not enough food for all of us! What is to become of us? What will happen to my poor children?'

'We have only one loaf of bread left,' said their stepmother. 'I have a plan. Let us take Hansel and Gretel out into the deepest part of the woods, give them some food and leave them alone. They will not be able to find their way back to the cottage, and maybe someone will look after them. Anyway, we shall be rid of them!'

'Oh, no, I could not do that,' said the woodcutter. 'How could I leave them alone in the woods? The wild beasts would tear them to pieces.'

But the woman argued and at last the man agreed to the plan. They didn't know that the two children had been so hungry they had not been able to sleep, and had heard all that was said.

Gretel wept bitterly, but Hansel comforted her. 'Don't cry, little sister,' he said. 'I'll think of something.'

Later, when all was quiet, he slipped out of the cottage in the moonlight and picked up some shiny white pebbles which

glittered like pieces of silver.

    'Go to sleep, little Gretel, I will look after you,' he said when he returned, and they soon fell asleep.

Next morning the children's stepmother roused them early. 'We are going to the forest to gather wood,' she told them and she gave them each a piece of bread. Gretel put both pieces in her pocket, for Hansel's pocket was full of stones.

The family set out for the forest, but Hansel kept looking back over his shoulder. He did it so often that his father noticed and asked him what he was doing.

'Oh, Father,' said Hansel, 'I am looking at my little white kitten, who is sitting on the roof to wave goodbye.'

'You stupid boy,' said his stepmother, 'that is not your kitten, but the sun on the chimney pot.'

Of course, Hansel had not been looking for his kitten. He had dropped a pebble every now and then, all along the path.

When they came to the middle of the forest, their father told them to find wood to light a fire. Hansel and Gretel gathered up some brushwood and made a huge pile in a clearing. Their father soon had a merry blaze burning, and their stepmother told the children to rest by its warmth.

'We are going into the forest to cut some more wood, and we will come back for you later,' she told them.

Hansel and Gretel sat by the warm fire and ate their bread. They could hear their father's axe nearby as he chopped the trees, but the sound grew fainter and fainter. They were very tired, and, soothed by the warmth of the fire, they fell asleep. When they woke up it was dark and Gretel, who was very frightened, began to cry.

'How can we get out of this wood?' she sobbed. 'We shall be lost for ever.'

'Wait a little while,' said Hansel, 'and the moon will come up and we can find our way home.'

At last the full moon rose, and Hansel took his sister by the hand and they followed the trail of pebbles. It was not long before they came in sight of the cottage.

'You bad children!' cried their stepmother, opening the door. 'Why did you stay so long in the forest?' Just as if she had been expecting them. But their father was very glad to see them.

A few days later there was again no food in the house and at night Hansel and Gretel heard their stepmother say that they would have to take them into the woods once more. Hansel found the door locked, so he could not go out and pick up some more shiny white pebbles, but he comforted Gretel by telling her he would think of something.

Next morning the family rose early and the woman gave the children a piece of bread. As they set off into the forest Hansel again kept stopping and looking back over his shoulder. On the way to the wood he broke off little pieces of bread and dropped them in the pathway to guide them home later.

'What are you looking at?' asked his father.

'I am looking at my little pigeon, sitting on the roof saying goodbye to me,' answered Hansel.

'You stupid boy,' said his stepmother, 'that is not your pigeon, but the sun on the chimney pots.'

The woodcutter led the children far, far into the wood, where they had never been in all their lives. He made a large fire, and the stepmother said, 'Sit down and rest now, and eat your bread. We are going to chop wood and will come back for you later.'

So Gretel shared her piece of bread with Hansel and soon they fell asleep again by the fire.

It was night when they woke up and the fire had died down. Gretel began to cry, but Hansel put his arm round her and told her to wait until the moon rose. 'We shall see our way home then,' he said, 'just as we did before.'

The moon rose, bright and clear, but this time they could find no trace of the crumbs Hansel had dropped on the way to the forest. The birds of the forest had eaten them all up.

'Never mind,' said Hansel bravely, 'we shall soon find the right path.'

Hand in hand they set off along the twisty, winding forest trails. Gretel was scared when, out of the dark, tree branches brushed her face, but Hansel told her not to be afraid, he was sure he would find the way home.

They wandered all night, all next day and the next, but they could not find a path out of the wood. They were very hungry, for all they had eaten were a few berries. They sat under a great oak tree and fell asleep.

At noon, when they woke up, they saw a pretty white bird, perched on a branch and singing a sweet song. They stopped to listen, and then it flew towards them and flapped its wings, as if to tell them to follow it. So they walked down a little path and on and on until they came to a little house, and the bird sat on the rooftop watching them.

'What a funny house!' said Gretel.

'It looks good enough to eat,' said Hansel, and they stood and stared.

38

They had never seen such a strange house. The cottage was made of gingerbread, covered with little fairy cakes, and the windows were glistening sugar. One of the chimneys was made of ginger snaps.

'Now we can eat all we want,' said Hansel, breaking off a piece of the wall and cramming it into his mouth. Soon he and Gretel were eating all they could break off the house.

Suddenly, from inside the house, a shrill voice called out,

'Nibble, nibble, little mouse,
Who is nibbling at my house?'

And the children answered,

'Never mind,
It is the wind,'

and went on eating. Hansel was busily eating the roof, and tore down a huge piece of it, while Gretel pushed out a big, round window-pane and sat down to enjoy it. Suddenly the door opened and an old, bent woman hobbled out, leaning on a stick. Hansel and Gretel were very frightened and dropped the food they were eating. They huddled together in fear.

'Come, my dears, don't be afraid,' said the old woman. 'Come inside and tell me what you are doing in this part of the forest.'

The cottage was quite ordinary inside, with a bright hearth and fire burning, and a gleaming kettle on the hearth. The old woman told the children to sit at the table, and a big black cat rubbed itself against their legs while the old woman prepared a lovely meal of little pancakes and fruit. Later she took them upstairs to two little white beds, and soon Hansel and Gretel were fast asleep.

What the children did not know was that the old woman was a witch who had made the cottage just to entice them in, and that she had sent the white bird to bring them. She liked to eat children and Hansel and Gretel would make a fine feast for her. She rubbed her gnarled hands in glee and said to the black cat, 'He, he, he, what a feast we shall have with those two children. I must feed them up first, for they are a bit skinny now.'

Next morning, while they were still sleeping peacefully, the old witch grabbed Hansel from his bed and took him, struggling, to the yard outside, where she locked him into a cage. He screamed, but to no avail. He was a prisoner. Poor Gretel was very frightened and began to cry, but the old witch had no pity.

'Get up, you lazybones,' she called. 'Clean the house, fetch the water from the well, and cook a meal for your brother. When he is fat enough, I will eat him.'

Gretel wept bitterly, but it was no use. She had to do all the witch told her, and cleaned the house and cooked huge meals for Hansel, while she was only allowed to eat scrapings from the pot.

Every morning the old witch hobbled out into the yard and peered at Hansel. 'Stick your finger through the bars, Hansel,' she would order. 'Let me see how fat you are getting. Are you fat enough to eat yet?'

But Hansel always pushed a chicken bone through the bars instead of his finger and the old woman would feel it in her withered hand, and stare at it, and shake her head. 'Why doesn't he get any fatter?' she would mutter to herself.

After a month had passed the witch grew impatient and told Gretel to draw some water. 'Fat or thin, I shall eat him tomorrow,' she declared.

Gretel cried and cried, but she had to make up the fire and boil the water.

'First we will do some baking,' cried the old witch. 'Stoke up the oven and see that it is really hot.'

So Gretel fetched more wood and soon the flames were leaping and dancing in the stove.

'Now creep in and see if it is hot enough,' said the witch, meaning to roast Gretel so that she could eat her before she cooked Hansel.

'I don't know how to get in! What shall I do?' asked Gretel who had guessed the old woman's plans.

'You stupid girl,' snapped the old witch. 'Out of my way. I'll show you how to do it.' And she opened the oven door and leant forward to feel the heat.

Quickly, Gretel gave a shove and the old woman fell right in! With all her might Gretel pushed the door and fastened the iron bolt. How the witch howled! Gretel had never heard such a noise in her life, but she did not open the door, and all the witch's magic was powerless against the flames.

Gretel ran to the yard and let Hansel out of his prison. How they kissed and laughed now that they were free!

With the witch safely out of the way Hansel and Gretel went from room to room, and they soon found some boxes with pearls and precious stones. They filled some sacks, and Gretel filled her apron.

'Now let's get away from here,' said Hansel, and they set off into the forest.

45

After walking a long way they came to a huge lake. 'We can never get across,' said Hansel. 'There is no bridge, and no stepping stones.'

'And no boat either,' said Gretel. 'But here comes a white duck. Let's ask her if she will help us.

> *'Little duck, good little duck,*
> *Hansel and Gretel, here we stand.*
> *There is neither stile nor bridge*
> *Take us on your back to land.'*

So the duck came to the bank and Hansel sat on her back, telling Gretel to wait while he went across. It did not take long and soon both children had crossed the lake. They thanked the kindly duck and were on their way once more.

At last they came to a part of the forest they knew, and soon they were running down the path to their father's cottage.

'Father! Father! We're home!' they cried and the woodcutter opened the door and came to meet them, his arms held wide in welcome. He clasped them to him and they all laughed and cried at the same time. He had been very lonely since he left them in the forest, and he had often tried to find them in the deep woods. His wife had died, but now he and his children were together again.

'Look what we've brought,' cried Hansel and Gretel as they tipped up the sacks of precious stones and pearls on to the table, spilling them on to the floor as well.

From that day on, their troubles were over and they all lived happily ever after. But none of them ever went to find the gingerbread house again!

Rumpelstiltskin

Once upon a time there was a poor miller who had a beautiful daughter of whom he was very proud. He was always boasting about her, saying how clever she was and how she would make a fine queen.

One day the King was riding by and saw the girl, admiring her beauty. The miller was quick to notice this, and proudly told the King that his daughter was very clever.

'Why, she can spin straw into gold thread!' he boasted.

The King needed money for his armies, so he took the girl back to the palace where he locked her into a room filled with straw. A spinning wheel stood in the corner.

'Spin this into gold,' ordered the King. 'You have until sunrise to do it, but if your father lied to me, it will be the worse for you!' And he strode off, locking the door behind him.

The poor girl looked around her, first at the pile of straw and then at the spinning wheel. She knew she could not spin straw into gold and she was frightened. She began to cry. Then she heard a faint scratching sound, low down on the door. As she watched she saw the locked door opening, and a strange little man stood beside her.

'What is the matter?' he asked. 'Why do you weep?'

'I'm so unhappy,' the poor girl said. 'The King has commanded me to spin this straw into gold and I don't even

48

know how to spin!'

The little man scratched his head. 'What will you give me if I do it for you?' he asked.

'My necklace,' said the girl, taking it off.

The little man put the necklace in his pocket and sat down at the spinning wheel, and soon the room was filled with a whirring sound. The straw disappeared into bobbins of fine gold thread.

Next morning the King was delighted to see so much gold in place of the straw. But he was a greedy man, and wanted more. So he ordered the girl to stay in the palace, and she was taken to a bigger room filled to the rafters with more straw to spin into gold.

That night the poor girl began to cry again for she knew she could not spin the straw. Once again the little man appeared and asked, 'What will you give me if I spin this straw into gold for you?'

'The ring from my finger,' the girl replied and he slipped that too into his pocket. He sat down and the spinning wheel began to whirr, while the girl watched in amazement as the straw disappeared into bobbins of gold thread, even more shiny than the first ones.

But the King was not satisfied, and he took the girl to the biggest room she had ever seen. 'If you spin this straw into gold by sunrise, you can be my queen,' promised the King. He knew that the girl was both beautiful and clever, for already she had brought him much wealth.

Scarcely had he gone before the little man appeared. 'What will you give me this time?' he asked, looking at the straw.

'I have nothing left to give you,' said the girl weeping, for she was very frightened.

'Promise to give me your first child when you are Queen,' said the little man.

'Oh, yes, anything,' promised the girl, and soon the spinning wheel began to whirr. All night long the little man sat spinning and the bales of straw were turned into fine golden bobbins of thread. The girl was delighted.

Next day the King saw that she had fulfilled her task and he married her. They were very happy and the girl soon loved him very much. She was happy in the palace and there was great rejoicing when her son was born the following year. She had long forgotten all about the little man, but he remembered her promise.

Early one morning, when she was playing with her baby, he came to see her and reminded her of her promise. He held out his arms to take the child, but she clung to her baby, pleading with him not to take her son.

'I will give you all the riches in the kingdom,' she cried. 'But please leave my baby. I will give you all the gold you can carry!'

'Oh, no, I don't want your gold,' said the little man. 'I want your son.'

The Queen pleaded with him, tears falling on to her rich clothes. 'Please, please let me keep my son!' she begged, until at last the little man relented.

'Very well, you can keep your son, but only if you can guess my name in three days.' And he disappeared.

The Queen smiled for she was sure she would soon guess his name. She did not know that the little men did not have the same names as everyone else.

She sent for all the books her servants could carry and sat up all night looking for names for the little man. She began with the letter A and went right on through the alphabet.

Next day when the little man came to see her, the Queen asked him, 'Is your name Algernon, Balthazar or Caspar?' But he shook his head and danced with glee. She could not guess his name.

It was the same the following morning. He shook his head when she asked, 'Are you called Noah, Timothy or Marmaduke?'

The poor Queen was distracted. Somehow, she must find out the little man's name. She sent messengers all over the country to find out what other people called their children, and soon she had a list of names that stretched across the room. Somehow, she knew that none of them was the right one and she was very sad.

Very late in the afternoon of the last day, one of her messengers rode in. His clothes were dirty and mud-stained, and his cloak had been torn by brambles. He knelt before the Queen saying, 'Your Majesty, I have not found any new names, but as I rode over the mountain, I came to the edge of the wood where the fox says goodnight to the hare, and I saw a little, old cottage. In the garden, dancing round a fire which was burning brightly, was a little man. He was singing a strange song.'

'Can you remember the words?' the Queen interrupted, quivering with excitement.

'Yes,' said the messenger, 'he was singing a little song:

    "Today I brew, tomorrow I bake
    And next day the Queen's child I'll take.
    Little does she guess, poor dame,
    That Rumpelstiltskin is my name!"'

56

'Rumpelstiltskin! What a funny name,' said the Queen, but she was very happy, for she felt at once that this was the right name and that her child was saved.

The little man came in the morning and the Queen asked him, 'Is your name Roger?'

'No,' said the little man.

'Is it Henry, then?' asked the Queen.

'No, no, you'll never guess it,' screamed the little man. 'The child is mine!'

'Well, is it Rumpelstiltskin?' asked the Queen.

'The Devil has told you! The Devil has told you!' The little man jumped up and down with rage. 'Rumpelstiltskin *is* my name!' The little man was so angry he jumped and stamped his feet with such fury that he disappeared through the floor. And he was never seen again.

The Ugly Duckling

It was a lovely summer day, and a soft breeze stirred the clump of weeds that grew by the pond. The large, white duck sitting on a clutch of eggs stretched herself, shook out her feathers and then settled herself once more on to her nest. Hatching eggs was a long business, and she seemed to have been sitting there for ever!

The rest of the farm was quiet: a few bees busied themselves among the flower beds, some hens scratched about in the dust, not really looking for anything, and the old donkey blinked in the sunlight by the fence. The cows stood in silence, munching the lush grass, and the farm cat lay on the cobbles letting the sun's rays warm him.

Most of the ducks were swimming on the pond and no one bothered to go and talk to the duck sitting all alone on her nest. She looked across and heard them quacking and splashing and longed to join them. It should not be long now, but she did wish the ducklings would hurry and hatch out. And would you believe it? Just then they began to crack the eggs that had been their home for so long. 'Quack!' 'Quack!' First one, then another and another, the fluffy babies staggered out on to the grass, blinking a little in the bright sunlight. The mother duck was very pleased with her brood – six yellow ducklings, the prettiest she had ever seen! She turned and began to kick the broken eggshells

from the nest when she noticed there was one egg left. It was a large one, so maybe it took longer to hatch. Wearily, she sat down again and covered it with the soft down of her body. She watched the other ducklings as they waddled in the sunshine.

'Don't go too far away,' she told them.

Just then, another duck waddled up to talk to her.

'Oh, I see the ducklings have hatched out,' she said, looking at them. 'Fine little ones, aren't they? Why are you still sitting there?'

'There is one egg left,' said Mother Duck, getting up to show her. 'It's bigger than the rest.'

'I should leave it,' said her friend. 'It looks more like a turkey's egg than a duck's!'

'Oh, I can't leave my last egg – I'm sure it won't take long,' said Mother Duck, and she settled herself once more on the nest.

She had not long to wait. With a louder 'Quack' than the others, a grey, ugly scrap pushed its way out of the egg and frowned in the sunlight. It shook itself and looked around.

'My! You are ugly,' said Mother Duck. 'Still it can't be helped. Come along and meet your brothers and sisters, then we must go to the pond.'

Quacking and pushing, the other ducklings crowded round their new brother.

'Isn't he awful!' they cried, pecking at him. Soon, the poor little duck was hiding to keep away from their sharp beaks.

'Come along now,' said Mother Duck, 'enough of that. It's time for a swim.' And she led the way to the pond, the ducklings behind her, one after the other, with the odd, little grey one last of all.

The water felt cool, and soon Mother Duck and her brood were happily swimming around on it. She looked at her youngest. 'Oh, well, he's certainly not a turkey, that's for sure,' she said. 'He swims too well.'

At last she called them together and, one by one, they followed
her to the farmyard to pay their respects to the Queen of the
farmyard. This was a very old, very large duck who, as be-
fitting her special position, wore a red rag round her leg. All
the other ducks were scared of her, and she sat near the water's
edge, her quick eyes missing nothing all day long. Her word was
law among the ducks.

'I've brought the children to meet you,' said Mother Duck
pushing them forward.

'What's this one then?' quacked the old duck, looking at the
little grey one, huddling at the back.

'He was the last to hatch,' said Mother Duck. 'He was so long

in the egg I expect it made him a bit droopy.'

'Humph!' The old duck quacked to herself. 'Funny sort of duck if you ask me.' And she glided on to the cool water for a swim.

Soon all the other ducklings and chickens in the farmyard began to tease the ugly duckling, pecking at him and chasing him away. The old farm cat hissed at him, and the poor little bird ran away to dodge his claws.

At last he could bear it no longer and flew over the hedge into the next field, all the little sparrows and starlings flying up in fear as he passed. 'Oh dear, even other birds are frightened,' he said to himself. 'I must be the ugliest bird in the whole world.'

He found himself on the edge of a large lake. Up in the sky some large ducks with pretty coloured markings flew and squawked. When they saw him they flew down and looked at the stranger who had come to their lake. 'Who are you?' they asked him, poking him this way and that with their beaks.

'Oh, don't send me away,' he begged. 'Just let me hide here for a while.'

So they left him alone and he watched them swirling and flying high in the blue sky. Suddenly a loud bang frightened him. Then another and another, and two of the beautiful ducks fell to the ground near him. One more landed in the water with a loud splash, and soon the lake was red with its blood. The little duck looked on in horror. What was happening? There was a crash and the sound of breaking twigs, then a large black dog came through the weeds towards him. The little duck quivered with fright, but the dog looked at him and turned and ran away barking.

'Oh, even a dog is scared of my ugly face,' said the little duck. The banging went on until he could bear it no more, and he flew away over the hedge. At last he came to a tiny cottage by the side of a wood. It was very old, with a crooked chimney and a topsy-turvy roof.

In the doorway stood a very old woman with a black cat rubbing itself against her legs. In the garden a small brown hen clucked and scratched in the dust. The little duck, tired and panting from his flight, came up to the cottage.

'May I come in?' he asked timidly, and the old woman pushed open the door for him. He sat in a corner watching as she fed the cat and the hen.

'Do you lay eggs?' the old woman asked, and he shook his head.

'Can you purr like me?' asked the cat, and again he shook his head.

'So you are no use at all,' said the cat and began to chase him from the cottage. The hen pecked at him and then the old woman, cross at all the noise, shooed them all out into the garden. The little duck ran as fast as his legs would carry him.

So a lonely life began for the little duckling. No one would speak to him, so he hid by the lake all by himself. He swam on the clear water, he dived to the bottom, but the fish were too quick for him. He tried hard to make friends with the other creatures round the shore, but he was so ugly that no one wanted anything to do with him.

The days passed. The lazy, warm days of summer turned cool, and the autumn came. The leaves on the trees turned yellow, then brown and dry until, teased by the wind, they fell, making a scrunchy carpet on the ground. Some days the wind tossed them hither and thither, making the branches dance, and the little duck watched them in delight. They looked so pretty in the pale sunlight.

But winter was coming. The sky was heavy with rain and the old raven on the fence shook his feathers and shivered. The cold night air was eating into his bones.

One evening the little duck heard a strange sound. High above him, some large and beautiful birds were flying across the lake. He had never seen anything so majestic. They were shining white and had long, slender necks that stretched in front of them as they flew. Their cries sounded wild as, with their great wings extended, they flew overhead, away to a warmer land across the sea.

The little duck felt a sudden happiness. There was something so beautiful about those birds, and it was as if their cries had been for him. He quivered with excitement. How he would like to join them. If only he could fly away with them!

The winter came with a heavy fall of snow. The ice on the lake tingled and froze, and the little duck kept swimming and swimming to keep warm. Then one day all the water had frozen and he could not swim. He huddled in the weeds, too cold to move and at last his feet froze in the ice.

A farmer, passing by, noticed his plight. 'Why, you poor frozen little mite!' he said, and he picked up the little duck to take home to his children.

68

The warmth of the big kitchen thawed out the tiny body and the little duck flapped his wings. It was good to feel such heat!

The farmer's children wanted to play with him, but he was frightened of them and flew up in panic. He knocked over a bowl of milk which ran out in a white stream across the floor. The farmer's wife clapped her hands and the little duck jumped into the flour bin in terror. The children laughed, the woman shouted and the duck flew out and into the butter! What a mess he was in! There was noise and bustle everywhere, with the children shrieking, the farmer's wife clapping her hands and the little duck sticky with flour and butter. When the door opened he ran out into the garden and kept running until he found a quiet place in the soft snow.

The winter was long and hard and the poor little duck was cold, lonely and very sad. Somehow he managed to find food, but he was shivering in the weeds and very often there was not much to eat. At last the snow melted, the ice dissolved into clear, sparkling water and he felt the sun on his back. The fields were green again, the rabbits played in the woods and the trees put on their green leaves. Spring was here at last!

He tried his wings and found they were stronger. He soared high into the air, higher and higher, faster and faster. He felt free and alive. On and on he flew until he came to a large garden near an old grey-stoned house. It had pretty flowers and soft, green lawns, with a large, shining lake.

Then he saw a magical sight. Three graceful swans came gliding down the lake towards the house. How majestic they looked, white and gleaming in the soft spring sunlight!

The little duck looked at them. How proud and fine they were. He made up his mind. 'I will fly over to see these proud birds,' he said to himself, 'and they will peck me and that will be the end. It is better to die with birds like these than to live alone and unwanted. And I don't want to live through another cold winter like the last one.'

Bravely, he flew over to the lake, on and on towards the magnificent white birds. They saw him and flew towards him.

'Kill me,' he said meekly, bowing his head towards the water.

Then he had a wonderful surprise! Instead of the ugly, grey bird he had always seen, he was looking at a beautiful white swan! He blinked and looked again. It was true, he *was* a swan.

The beautiful birds crowded round him, laughing and talking. 'Where have you come from?' they asked, welcoming him. 'Where have you been all the winter?'

Just then, some children came into the park to feed the swans.

'Look, Mummy,' they called, 'there is a new swan! Isn't he lovely?'

'He's the most beautiful swan I have ever seen,' said a little girl, and threw him a large piece of bread.

The older swans laughed and nodded their tall necks in agreement.

'You are the most beautiful swan we have ever seen,' they said. 'Will you come and live here with us?'

The little swan, who had always thought he was an ugly duckling, felt his heart would burst with pride. All his dreams had come true and he was a magnificent swan. At last he was with his own kind – and no one would ever call him ugly again.

The Three Bears

Long, long ago three bears all lived together in a house deep in the forest. There was Father Bear who was big and rough and spoke with a gruff voice, and Mother Bear who was smaller, with a soft kindly voice and smooth, silky fur, and lastly there was Little Bear who was very small, like a ball of fluff. He had a squeaky voice.

The bears were a happy family. Each one had his own bed – Father Bear's was big and hard, Mother's smaller and soft, and Little Bear's was the most comfortable of all, and just right for him. Father Bear's chair was made of wood, and was very high; Mother's was in red velvet, and Little Bear had his own special chair with his name on it. They loved to eat porridge, and every day Mother Bear would heat up the big saucepan filled with their favourite food, and pour some into each bowl.

One day it was fine, with the sun shining, and the porridge was too hot to eat at once, so the three bears decided to go for a walk while it cooled.

There also lived in the forest a little girl who was called Goldilocks because of her fair hair. She loved to go exploring, and one day she came to the bears' house.

'How quaint it looks!' she cried, peeping inside the gleaming windows. She could see the table with the three chairs in a row and the bowls of steaming porridge.

'Is anybody at home?' she called out. But no one answered. She was very curious so she tried the door handle. It opened. Goldilocks pushed the door and went inside. There was no one there so she went exploring.

'What a funny house!' she laughed, looking all round her. The three chairs stood in a row near the fire and Goldilocks sat in Father Bear's, nearest the fire.

'My, you are hard!' she cried, jumping off and sitting in Mother Bear's chair with the red velvet cover.

'You are much softer,' said Goldilocks, 'but I keep slipping off.'

So she sat on Little Bear's chair. But she was far too heavy, and the chair broke in pieces on the floor.

Goldilocks saw the three bowls of porridge on the table. She picked up a spoon and dipped it into Father Bear's bowl. That was too hot and she burned her mouth. So she tried Mother Bear's but that was too cold! Then she tried Little Bear's and it was so good that she ate it all up.

Now she was feeling sleepy so she went upstairs. She found three beds, all in one room, each with its own patchwork cover. Father Bear's bed was too big and it was very hard. Goldilocks tried Mother Bear's but it was too soft and she didn't like it at all. Then she curled up on Little Bear's bed. This was just right and very soon she was fast asleep.

After a while the three bears came home from their walk. 'Mummy, look!' cried Little Bear, 'someone has been sitting on my chair, and it's all broken!'

'*Someone* has been sitting in my chair, too,' said Father Bear looking very fierce.

'And mine,' said Mother Bear. She wondered who it could be.

'Someone's been eating my porridge!' said Father Bear in a very cross voice. He had been looking forward to that porridge.

'And mine, too,' said Mother Bear, puzzled.

'They've eaten all mine up!' said Little Bear.

The three bears went upstairs. Father Bear soon found that someone had been sleeping on his bed. The cover was all crumpled. So was Mother Bear's. And then Little Bear cried out, 'Someone's been sleeping in my bed, and she's still there!'

The noise woke Goldilocks and she had a terrible fright when she saw three bears looking at her.

'Oh, my,' said Goldilocks. 'Three bears!' She was very scared, because the bears looked so cross.

'You have broken my chair and eaten all my porridge,' said Little Bear. He was very sad, for he liked his chair and he *loved* porridge.

'I'm sorry,' said Goldilocks. 'I was so hungry, and I didn't mean to break your chair. Truly I didn't.'

She ran down the stairs and out of the house as fast as her legs would carry her. All the way home, through the woods, she kept looking back to see if the bears were chasing her, but they had stayed at home. Goldilocks never went exploring again.

The Little Fir Tree

ar, far away deep in the forest there grew a little fir tree. The breeze played gently with his branches and the sun shone on him, and all around were other fir trees, some big and tall and others small and feathery. The little fir tree longed to grow up, it was all he wanted from life. He did not laugh at the breeze nor smile at the sun, nor listen to the singing and dancing of the children who played in the woods.

Sometimes the children came into the forest to look for wild strawberries, and, when they had found them, would sit underneath the little fir tree to eat them.

'What a lovely little tree he is!' they would say and touch his branches, pretending to tickle him.

This did not please the little tree at all. He wanted to grow tall and strong like the giant pines who towered over the forest. Year by year he grew, but though each year his trunk grew wider, he still longed to be able to stretch his branches for the birds to nest in, and to reach up to the blue sky high above him.

In the winter time, when the ground was covered with a white mantle of snow, the trees looked freshly green, the brilliant snow glistening on their branches like silver. Once a hare jumped right over the little tree, making him very cross. But when two more winters had passed the little tree had grown tall and the hare had to run round him.

The woodcutters came in the autumn and chopped down the
tallest trees. The little fir tree shivered when he heard the crack,
crack of the axes in the forest, and winced when he heard the
tearing and crashing as a big tree fell. The men would cut off the
fine branches, and the great trunks lay bare on the ground. The
wagons came and they were loaded up and pulled away by the
strong, brown horses. Where are they going? What happens to
them? The little tree wondered and shook.

In the spring, when the swallows returned to the forest, the little fir tree asked them, 'Where do the old trees go? Have you seen them again?'

The swallows could tell him nothing, but a wise old stork nodded her head and told him, 'I think I know. I saw many new ships with tall, straight masts as I flew over Egypt. I expect the trees are made into masts for these ships – they had the scent of pine about them. They were so grand!'

'Oh, if only I were big enough to sail the seas,' the little fir tree sighed. 'What is the sea? What is it like?'

'Oh, it would take a lifetime to tell you,' said the stork. 'Be happy here in the forest. Enjoy the sunbeams that dance on your branches. You will grow up all too soon.' And she flew away to perch high in one of the tallest trees.

The wind blew gently over the tree and the dew dropped its coldness as if to say it understood, but the little tree was sad.

The woodcutters returned just before Christmas and began to cut down many of the smaller trees in the forest. They were very careful not to hurt the branches and laid them all in little carts to be taken away by the horses.

'Where do the little trees go?' the little fir tree wondered. They could not be masts for tall ships, so where did they go?

'We can tell you!' twittered the sparrows. 'We have seen them! Down in the city we have peeked in at the windows of the houses, and seen the trees! They are so beautiful! You cannot imagine what honour and glory they are given! We have seen them in a warm room, with the firelight glowing, and decorated with little silver bells, tiny packets of sweets and special little toys. Oh, and there were hundreds of tiny candles which flickered and twinkled all the time. You have never seen such wonderful trees!'

'And then?' asked the little tree. 'What happens then?'

'That was so wonderful, we did not look for anything else,' the sparrows answered.

The birds twittered and the little fir tree grew very excited. 'Shall I be dressed like that one day?' he wondered. 'It might be better than growing into a tall, tall mast for a ship. Oh, how I would love to be in a room, dressed with pretty things and everyone would come and admire me. Oh, how I wish I were grown up!'

'Be happy in the sunshine,' called the other trees. 'Do not always wish to be in another place, doing other things.'

But the little fir tree sulked. He wanted more than anything to be a special party tree. He went on growing and at last he was fresh and green and just right to be cut down for a Christmas tree.

He was the first to be cut down. He was surprised to feel the sharp tap of the axe and he fell to the ground, bruised and sore. Suddenly he felt sad at leaving the forest and his friends, but it was too late. Soon he was lying with a lot of other trees, dazed and raw, being jolted along the dusty road in the back of a cart. The little tree did not enjoy it at all!

At last he was free, and a man shook out his branches and looked at him. 'This is a good one,' he said to his helper. 'It should make a high price.' And he stacked the little tree against the wall in his yard.

The little tree stood there, wondering what would happen next, when he heard a man's voice saying, 'This is the one I want! I'll send someone to pick it up,' and he felt the shopkeeper tie a label round his trunk.

Later two smartly dressed footmen in livery, with shiny silver buckles and powdered wigs carried him through the town and up the steps of a fine house. The little tree was very excited. Soon he would be beautiful.

The men placed the little fir tree in a huge tub filled with yellow sand which tickled his trunk, and pushed him into a corner near the window. He looked round the room for the first time and saw that it was very large, with pictures on the walls, and on the mantelpiece were two huge Chinese vases with lions on their lids. There were sofas covered in blue brocade, tables piled high with picture books, and dozens of toys. A large grey and white rocking horse nearby nodded his head as if he approved of the little fir tree.

The little tree began to tremble. What would happen now? Two men and a young lady came into the room, their arms full of wondrous things. First of all, they hung on him little, brightly coloured baskets made of gay paper, each one full of sugar almonds, so that the little tree could feel them bounce. Shiny, polished apples were tied on, the firelight glowing and making them reflect the little clusters of nuts which were alongside, almost as if they were growing. Here and there they placed little, strange-shaped parcels with tiny labels on them. Then the great moment came. Dozens of little candles were fixed in the special holders near the tips of the branches, and, one by one, they were lit. The children came in and clapped their hands and danced round. They were so excited and happy and the little fir tree glowed with pride. He had never known such joy in his life!

Later a lady came into the room and, after climbing up the stepladder, she fixed a silver star at the very top of the little fir tree.

'There,' she said, 'now we are ready for Christmas.'

The little tree wondered if the sparrows would come and look at him through the windows. Would he stand there for ever, winter and summer, for everyone to admire his finery? But soon his branches began to ache for he was not used to all the weight pulling them down, and his bark was tingling. He shook himself and felt a burning as one of the candles singed him.

'Oh dear,' cried the lady, 'we must be careful!' And she blew out all the candles. The children sighed and she promised to light them again on Christmas Day.

The little fir tree dared not shake himself again, nor even tremble in case they did not light the candles.

Next day was Christmas Day and the candles were lit and the little fir tree shone in all his glory. He had not known it would be like this and he stretched with pride. Then, to his surprise, the candles burned low and were put out, and the children came to take their presents from the tree. They ripped off the parcels with delighted cries and soon the little tree was almost bare, with some of his greenery lying on the floor.

At last the children grew silent and gathered round the fire while their mother told them stories. The little fir tree listened to many fairy tales until it was time for bed.

Next morning, very early, just as the sun was peeping over the house-tops, the servants came in. The little tree blinked, and thought to himself, 'Ah, they are going to decorate me again for another day!' He was wrong. Very, very wrong.

One of them pulled him roughly out of the tub and carried him upstairs to a large, dirty room with a tiny skylight. He propped the tree against the wall and left him alone. The little tree looked around. The room was full of old, dusty things. There was a toy horse with one leg missing, several broken chairs, a horsehair sofa with the hair falling all over the floor, and a lot of large boxes. 'What a strange room,' thought the little tree. He did not like it at all. It seemed as if everyone had forgotten him.

Once a man came in and pushed some trunks into a dark corner, but he did not look at the tree.

'It is winter now,' thought the little tree, 'it is very cold, and the forest must be covered with crisp, white snow. I suppose they cannot plant me now as the ground is too hard, so I must wait here until the spring comes.' He felt very lonely.

Some mice began scampering all around him, talking and playing. The little tree did not like them very much. He wanted to be outside again.

'Isn't it lovely and warm here?' the mice said, scampering all over his boughs.

'Where do you come from?' they asked him and he began to tell them of the forest and the hare who jumped over him. As he talked, he thought of the lovely forest where he should have been happy but where he was always discontented and he began to cry.

'Tell us more,' begged the mice and he told them some of the fairy tales he heard on the happiest night of his life when he had shone with all the little candles glowing and the children dancing and playing round him.

So the days passed and spring came again, the sun filtering into the tiny attic window. A servant came to tidy up the room and, after sweeping and dusting, picked up the little fir tree and carried him downstairs.

'At last,' thought the little tree to himself, 'they are going to plant me in the garden. My branches will grow fresh and green and I shall be beautiful again.'

The little tree stretched up to breathe the fresh, clean air and he heard the birds singing as they flew in and out of the trees. It was a lovely day and he was very happy.

The children were playing in the garden and they rushed up to the tree. 'Look! There's the silver star,' they cried pulling it off the top and they began stamping on the tree, snapping the branches. 'Pooh, it's all brown and old,' they said, leaving him on the ground. He began to wish he had been left in the attic.

One of the gardeners came and chopped the little fir tree into small pieces, and piled them up. Then he took a match and set fire to them. How the crisp, dry wood crackled and burned! The little tree sighed deeply, and each sigh was like a little shot. As he sighed, the little tree thought of the cool, green forest, how it glistened in the winter's snow, or was fresh and bright after a shower of rain. What a sad end for the poor little fir tree.

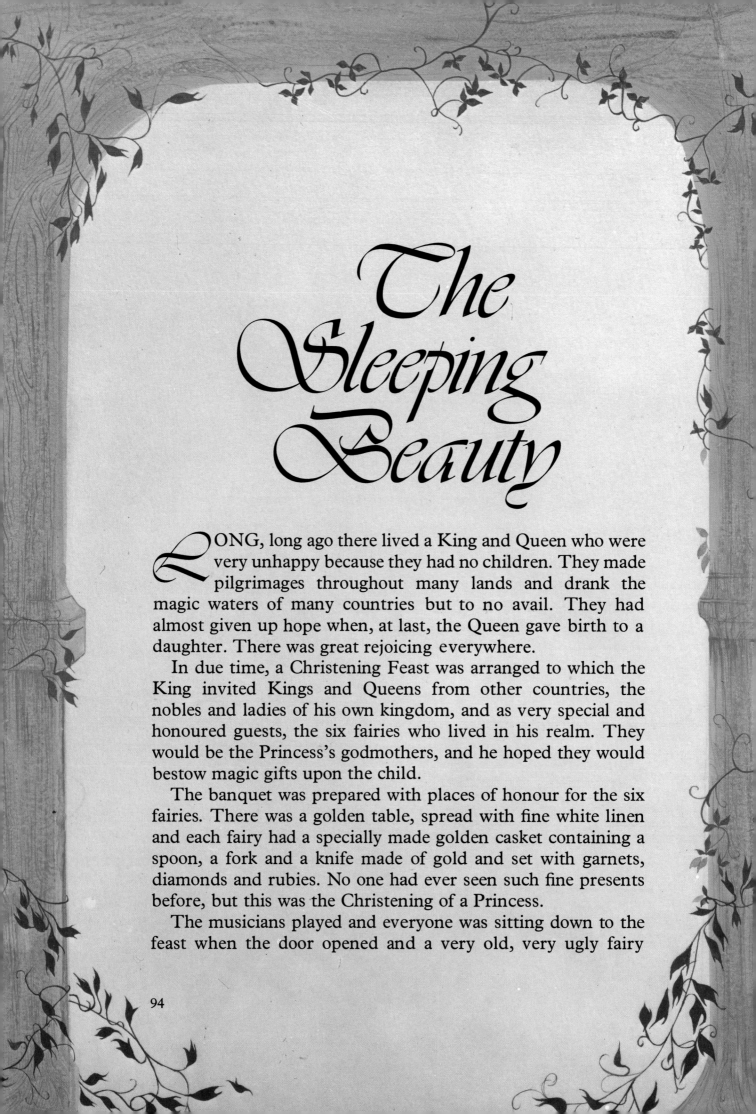

The Sleeping Beauty

LONG, long ago there lived a King and Queen who were very unhappy because they had no children. They made pilgrimages throughout many lands and drank the magic waters of many countries but to no avail. They had almost given up hope when, at last, the Queen gave birth to a daughter. There was great rejoicing everywhere.

In due time, a Christening Feast was arranged to which the King invited Kings and Queens from other countries, the nobles and ladies of his own kingdom, and as very special and honoured guests, the six fairies who lived in his realm. They would be the Princess's godmothers, and he hoped they would bestow magic gifts upon the child.

The banquet was prepared with places of honour for the six fairies. There was a golden table, spread with fine white linen and each fairy had a specially made golden casket containing a spoon, a fork and a knife made of gold and set with garnets, diamonds and rubies. No one had ever seen such fine presents before, but this was the Christening of a Princess.

The musicians played and everyone was sitting down to the feast when the door opened and a very old, very ugly fairy

94

entered leaning on a stick. She was dressed all in black and was very angry.

'You did not invite me!' she shrieked, waving her stick at the King and Queen.

'But, we, we . . .' the King stammered. The truth was that no one had seen the fairy for so long, they all thought she was dead, and they had forgotten all about her.

96

Hastily, the King ordered that a place be prepared for her with the other fairies, but, of course, there was no golden casket or knife, fork or spoon for her. The old fairy felt she had been slighted and muttered threats and curses as she picked at the feast. One of the young fairies, who sat next to her, listened to her grumbling. She thought the old fairy might give the baby Princess an unlucky gift, so she hid behind some curtains. She hoped she would be the last to make her gift and would be able to mend any evil the old fairy might do.

One by one, the fairies came to the Princess to offer their gifts. The youngest wished that the child should be the most beautiful Princess in the whole world; the next that she should have the nature of an angel; the third that she should have grace and the fourth that she should dance to perfection. The fifth wished that she should sing like a nightingale.

Then it was the turn of the old fairy. Shaking with rage, and leaning heavily on her stick, she pointed a bony finger at the sleeping Princess and declared:

'One day, you will pierce your hand on a spindle and die!'

A shudder of horror ran through the company, and it was then the young fairy stepped from behind the curtains.

'Take heart,' she said to the weeping King and Queen, 'the Princess will not die. It is true that I have no power to break the evil fairy's spell, and your daughter will prick herself with a spindle when she is fifteen. But, instead of dying, she will fall into a very deep sleep that will last for a hundred years. When that time has passed, a King's son will come and wake her.'

98

The King, trying to avert the terrible fate decreed by the bad fairy, ordered that every spindle in the kingdom be destroyed. On pain of death, he forbade anyone to use a spinning wheel or keep a spindle in their homes. So all spinning ceased and the wheels were silent.

The years passed happily and the wicked fairy's decree was forgotten. One day, when the Princess was fifteen, she and her parents were visiting one of their castles in the country. The young Princess was running about, exploring all the rooms, for she had never been there before. It was all a new adventure for her and she laughed as she ran from place to place.

At last she saw a tiny, twisting stairway that led up to a small garret at the top of the tower. Quickly, she ran up the stairs and stopped outside a door. She could hear a strange, whirring sound. Inside, an old woman sat spinning. She had not heard the King's orders forbidding the use of spinning wheels.

'Oh, what are you doing?' asked the Princess, coming into the room and watching the old woman.

'I am spinning, child,' said the old woman. She did not recognise the Princess.

'Oh, what is that?' asked the Princess, 'no one has told me of such a thing. How do you do it? Please let me try.'

The old woman handed her the spindle. No sooner had she picked it up, than she pricked her hand and fell into a deep sleep.

The old woman was very alarmed. She cried out for help and people came running from all over the castle. They threw water on the Princess's face, they rubbed her hands, they undid her clothes and even bathed her face with sweet-smelling perfume. But it was all to no avail. Nothing would waken her and she continued to sleep.

The King and Queen hurried back to their home, taking the sleeping Princess with them. The King ordered that she be placed in her bedchamber, on a bed embroidered with gold and silver.

The Princess looked beautiful lying asleep on her bed. Her sleep had not taken the colour from her cheeks which were pink and her lips were a pale coral. Although her eyes were closed, she still breathed gently, so they knew she was not dead. Her father ordered that she be left to sleep quietly until the spell be broken.

The good fairy, who had saved the life of the Princess by putting her to sleep, was out of the kingdom when the evil fairy's spell came true. A little dwarf, wearing seven league boots, came to tell her and she rode at once to the castle in a fiery chariot drawn by dragons.

'Everything is just right,' she said, looking round and trying to comfort the King and Queen. Then she suddenly thought that the Princess would feel lonely when she woke up and she picked up her magic wand. Gently, she tapped everyone in the castle—all the ladies and gentlemen of the court, the governesses, the officers, the stewards, the pages, the footmen, the guards, even the cooks, scullions, pantry boys and gardeners. Outside, she touched all the fine horses in the stable, the great watchdogs and little Mopsey, the Princess's pet dog. He climbed on to his mistress's bed and curled up at the foot of it.

Everyone fell asleep at once. The whole castle was silent, even the logs on the fire stopped burning and the chickens turning on the spits were still. The King and Queen kissed their daughter and the fairy touched them with her wand.

A great silence fell; time stood still. Within a few minutes of the enchantment, a great forest of enormous trees with bushes and briars sprang up all round the castle hiding it from sight. So no one would see the sleeping Princess until it was time for the spell to be broken.

A hundred years passed. One day the son of the reigning King (for a different family ruled the kingdom) was out hunting. He asked what the towers were he could just see peeping out of a great wood.

'It's a ruined old castle,' said one courtier.

'It's the home of an ogre who steals children,' said another. The Prince did not know what to think until he asked a very old peasant.

'Your Highness,' he said, 'more than fifty years ago, I heard my father tell that the most beautiful Princess in the world lies in that castle. She must sleep for a hundred years and only a King's son can wake her.'

The young Prince was filled with excitement. He had to see if the legend were true and if there really was a beautiful Princess asleep in the castle. Picking up his sword, he began to cut a way through the forest of trees, bushes and briars, but scarcely had he begun to do so, than they parted for him and the way was clear. Alone he rode on to the castle and came to the great fore-court. Looking about, he was filled with an icy terror. There was a terrible silence and the face of death all around him. Men, women and animals all appeared to be dead. It was very strange, for even the cups they held were filled with wine, and not a drop had spilt.

Bravely, the Prince pushed open the great door and climbed up a wide staircase. Here, everyone was fast asleep. Every room was the same. At last, he came to a room lined with gold. The curtains of the bed were pulled back and, lying on a bed embroidered with gold and silver, was the most beautiful girl he had ever seen. At the foot of the bed, a small dog slept peacefully.

The Prince put out his hand and touched her face, but she did not move.

'Do wake up,' he whispered and fell on his knees by the bed.

Just then, the enchantment ended, and the Princess fluttered her eyelids. 'Is that you my Prince?' she asked, 'I have waited a long time.'

The Prince was delighted, and bent and kissed her, and told her he loved her. Then, the spell was completely broken at last and everyone in the castle woke up and there was a great noise. The dogs barked, the horses neighed and the people chattered such as you have never heard before.

The King and Queen came to greet their daughter and saw that the fairy's words had come true. A Prince had woken her from her enchanted sleep.

Life at the castle went on as if it had not stopped for a hundred years. In the kitchen, the cook cuffed the kitchen boy for not turning the spit fast enough and the musicians played, the music sweeter than it had ever sounded before.

The Prince and Princess were married in the castle chapel and lived happily ever after.

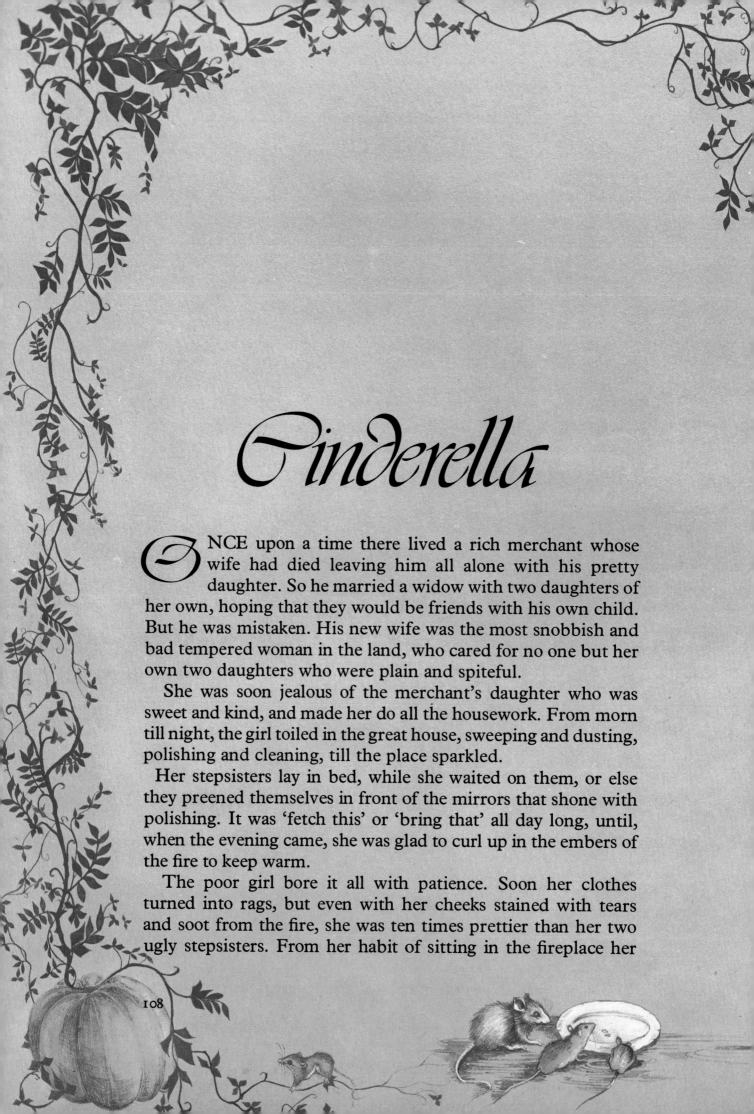

Cinderella

ONCE upon a time there lived a rich merchant whose wife had died leaving him all alone with his pretty daughter. So he married a widow with two daughters of her own, hoping that they would be friends with his own child. But he was mistaken. His new wife was the most snobbish and bad tempered woman in the land, who cared for no one but her own two daughters who were plain and spiteful.

She was soon jealous of the merchant's daughter who was sweet and kind, and made her do all the housework. From morn till night, the girl toiled in the great house, sweeping and dusting, polishing and cleaning, till the place sparkled.

Her stepsisters lay in bed, while she waited on them, or else they preened themselves in front of the mirrors that shone with polishing. It was 'fetch this' or 'bring that' all day long, until, when the evening came, she was glad to curl up in the embers of the fire to keep warm.

The poor girl bore it all with patience. Soon her clothes turned into rags, but even with her cheeks stained with tears and soot from the fire, she was ten times prettier than her two ugly stepsisters. From her habit of sitting in the fireplace her

stepsisters called her Clinkerlump, but the younger sister, who wasn't *quite* so unkind, sometimes called her Cinderella.

So the days passed and while the stepsisters grumbled and groused, for nothing was ever right for them, Cinderella still smiled as she worked.

One day there was great excitement in the merchant's house. A herald from the castle brought them an invitation to a grand ball which the King was giving in honour of his son's birthday. All the nobility and people of importance from round and about were to be invited, including the stepsisters because they were rich and well known.

They were very happy and excited at the thought of going to the castle and meeting the Prince who was known to be very handsome. All day long they looked at fine materials, and the bundles of silks, satins and rich velvets lay all round the house until the merchant began to grumble at the sight of them. But still the stepsisters could not make up their minds! Everything had to be right for this special occasion. Cinderella had excellent taste so her sisters asked her advice, which she gave freely.

At last the elder sister made up her mind. 'I shall wear red velvet with a lace trimming,' she announced, 'and I must have new red shoes to match.'

'Well, I shall wear a silk skirt with a gold-flowered cloak,' said her sister, 'and my diamond necklace will be just right.'

So the dressmakers and shoemakers were called in and the needles flew. At last the dresses were ready and Cinderella thought they were beautiful. But they did not please the sisters, who found fault with them, and she had to alter this, and sew that until they were satisfied.

On the day of the ball, Cinderella ran from one to the other helping them into their finery. The hairdressers came and piled their hair on top of their heads in the fashion of the day, while the sisters complained that this curl was too long, or this one too short. In the end, it was Cinderella who brushed and smoothed their hair to their satisfaction, and at last they were ready. They looked magnificent.

The younger sister, taking a last look in the mirror, said, 'Wouldn't you like to go to the ball, Cinderella?'

'Don't laugh at me,' begged Cinderella, 'I have no place there.'

'Yes, that's true,' said her cruel sister, 'everyone would laugh to see a Clinkerlump at the ball!'

Cinderella hung her head and said nothing. She helped them into their carriage, laughing and excited, and watched them out of sight down the road to the castle. Then she returned to the kitchen, and, sitting among the embers of the fire, she began to cry.

All at once there was a sudden light in the room! Startled, Cinderella looked up. Then she saw a shining figure standing beside her, glowing and beautiful.

'Don't be afraid, child,' the lady said gently. 'I am your fairy godmother. Why are you crying?'

'I should like . . . Oh, what's the use?' said Cinderella and could not stop her tears.

'You want to go to the ball, don't you?' asked her fairy godmother.

'Yes, yes,' sobbed Cinderella.

'Very well, so you shall!' said her fairy godmother. 'Do just as I tell you. Go into the garden and bring me the biggest pumpkin you can find.'

Drying her eyes, Cinderella went out and cut the largest pumpkin in the patch and brought it to her godmother. She could not see how a pumpkin would get her to the ball, but she watched as her godmother scraped all the seeds out, then touched it with her magic wand. It turned into a golden coach!

'Good, now for the horses to pull it,' said her godmother. 'If you look in the mousetraps, you will find six white mice. Bring them to me.'

As she was bid, Cinderella found the mousetraps. There were six white mice which she gave to her godmother. As the trap was gently lifted and each mouse ran out, she touched it with her magic wand and it turned into a prancing horse. Soon, there was a team of six white horses in front of the coach.

'Now for the coachman,' ordered her godmother. 'Go and look in the rat trap.'

The rat trap held a large, fat rat with fine whiskers. With a tap of the wand, it was transformed into a splendid coachman with twinkling eyes and the best whiskers you have ever seen.

'All we need now are the footmen,' said Godmother. 'In the garden shed, hiding by the watering can, you will see six lizards. Bring them to me.'

Cinderella was too happy to argue and soon the lizards turned into six footmen with snow-white breeches and blue velvet coats. They looked magnificent, just as if they had been born footmen.

'Well, there you are,' said the fairy godmother, 'you can go to the ball. Hurry up and get ready.'

'But how can I go in these rags?' asked Cinderella, holding out her tattered skirt.

Laughing, the fairy godmother touched Cinderella gently with her wand. At once the rags fell away and Cinderella was wearing a beautiful dress of gold and silver that sparkled as she moved. There was a necklace of diamonds in her hair to catch the light. Cinderella could not believe her eyes – this was truly a magic dress.

'Here are the slippers,' said her godmother holding out the daintiest, prettiest pair of glass slippers in the world. Cinderella gasped. 'Is this really happening?' she asked.

'Of course, now hurry along and enjoy yourself,' said her godmother kissing her, 'but whatever you do, do not stay after midnight. My magic will not last after then and everything will be as before. As soon as the clock strikes, you will be in rags.'

'I'll remember,' promised Cinderella and climbed into her coach.

The night was alive with stars which twinkled like tiny lights, and as the coach approached the castle on the hilltop, Cinderella could hear the faint echo of music and see the flickering shadows cast by the lanterns that swung from the walls.

When the Prince heard that a great and beautiful Princess had arrived in a magnificent coach, he came to greet her and led her to the ballroom. The music stopped and everyone stared at Cinderella. No one had ever seen anyone so beautiful. 'Who is she?' they whispered among themselves, but no one knew the answer.

Cinderella danced with the Prince, who could not take his eyes off her and would dance with no one else. A magnificent supper was served, but the Prince ate nothing, he just wanted to gaze at his Princess. Cinderella sat near her sisters and even offered them a dish of tiny, sugared fruit, but they did not recognise her.

So the evening wore on and the Prince and Cinderella danced and danced to the music forgetting the time. Then she heard the first stroke of midnight. She made a deep curtsey to the King and Queen, and ran down the steps and out of the castle, heedless of the Prince's shouts for her to come back.

As she reached the last few steps she could hear the clock striking. 'Boom! Boom! Boom!' In her haste, she dropped one of her slippers, but dared not stop to pick it up. The clock stopped and Cinderella was once more in rags, the coach and horses gone, though she did see a large rat slinking away into the darkness. Swiftly, she ran home to await her sisters' return.

They could talk of nothing but the ball and the beautiful Princess who had danced with the Prince all evening!

At the castle, the Prince was desolate. No one had seen his Princess leave and the servants said they had seen only a kitchen maid in rags by the gates. He held the slipper in his hands. Somehow he must find his Princess. The King had an idea. 'Why not send the heralds out to seek the owner of the slipper?' he suggested, 'and then you will find the Princess.'

120

So the heralds went out into the land carrying the glass slipper. Every girl must try it on, and the Prince would marry the one who could wear it. Every house in the kingdom was visited and every woman tried on the slipper, but to no avail. On the third day, the Prince himself accompanied the heralds and they came at last to the merchant's house. The stepsisters tried to squeeze their feet into the tiny slipper. The elder, seeing her toe was too large, thought of cutting it off, but her sister, impatient for her try, snatched it just in time. The younger sister had no luck either, her heel stuck out by several inches!

'Is there anyone else in the house?' asked the heralds.

'Let me try,' said Cinderella, who had been watching in the background. Her sisters laughed and mocked her, but the Prince was insistent. Even in her rags, he could see she was beautiful.

Cinderella sat down and slipped her foot into the tiny slipper. It fitted her beautifully. The two sisters were astonished and could not believe their eyes, but Cinderella put her hand in her pocket and brought out the second slipper.

At that very moment, her fairy godmother arrived and, touching Cinderella with her wand, changed her rags once more into the magnificent ball dress she had worn at the Castle.

The two sisters recognised the Princess and begged her forgiveness, and Cinderella kissed them and took them to the castle with her.

The Prince was overjoyed. He had found his Princess. In a few days they were married and lived happily ever after.

The Golden Goose

THERE was once a woodcutter who lived with his wife and three sons in a small cottage on the edge of a great forest. The youngest boy was nicknamed 'Dummling' or 'Simpleton', because he was stupid. Everything he did turned out badly, no matter how he tried, and his brothers jeered at him all day long.

His parents were just the same. 'Our youngest is a fool and no mistake,' his mother would sigh, and give him a burnt piece of cake for his tea. Dummling never seemed to mind though, and was always happy and smiling.

One day the woodcutter had to cut down one of the very tallest fir trees growing in the forest. There it stood, its branches stretching out to the winds, the topmost ones reaching for the blue sky. But it had to come down all the same.

The eldest son said he would do the job for his father. His mother packed him a special lunch bag with some rich fruit cake she had just baked and a bottle of her best wine in case he felt thirsty.

He soon found the tree because his father had marked it with a big white cross. He took a look at it, but being a lazy boy,

124

decided to eat his lunch before cutting it down. He found a
nice, shady bank and settled himself comfortably. The wine
was cool and refreshing and he was soon tucking into a big slice
of the cake. Then he saw a little, old, grey-bearded man coming
along the path towards him.

'Good morning,' said the little man politely. 'I see you have a fine lunch, and it's a long time since I had a bite to eat or anything to drink. Will you share your cake and wine with me?'

'What an idea!' said the woodcutter's eldest son. 'Certainly not. I have never seen you before, I don't know you and I don't want to know you,' he added rudely. 'Besides, I need all the cake and wine for myself.'

The little old man looked at him hard for a moment, then he disappeared into the forest.

When the woodcutter's son took up his axe to cut down the tree, the axe slipped and cut his arm! The wound was so deep he had to give up work and return home. There he was fussed over by his mother, and he did not work again for weeks.

Then the woodcutter asked his second son to go and cut down the tree for him.

'Of course,' said the lad, full of confidence. 'I will take more care, and have the tree down in no time.'

His mother wrapped a fine, nutty cake for him that she had baked that morning, and gave him some wine to drink.

When the second son reached the tree, he took one glance and sat down to eat before beginning his task. He took out the cake and the wine, and was just about to start his meal when he saw a little, old, grey-bearded man coming along the path towards him.

'Good morning to you,' said the little man. 'Will you share your food with me? It's a very long time since I had a bite to eat or anything to drink.'

'Clear off,' said the second son rudely, 'I won't share my food with anyone. Be off with you!'

The little old man looked at him hard, then he disappeared into the forest, shaking his head as he went.

Soon, his meal finished, the second son began work on the tree. As he lifted the axe, he thought of the little old man. 'Fancy expecting me to give him some of my cake,' he said to himself, 'when I have finished this tree, I shall need ten cakes.' At first it was easy, and soon a pile of wood chips lay on the ground beside him. Then suddenly the axe slipped, cutting his leg so badly that he could scarcely drag himself home.

Dummling had watched his brothers go to the woods. He wanted to help his father, but knew that he would be laughed to scorn. Now was his chance!

'Father, let me try,' he begged, 'I am sure I can cut down the tree for you.'

'Well, your brothers could not do it, so I am sure you can't, but a day in the forest won't hurt you. You'll learn sense when you cut yourself – but don't cut your head off,' he added laughing.

Dummling was very pleased although his mother did not bake a special cake for him. 'There's a piece of bread on the shelf,' she said, 'and here's some beer to wash it down.'

Dummling set off down the path whistling to himself. He found the tree, and a little, old, grey-bearded man was standing beside it.

'Good morning,' the little man said, 'I see you have some food with you. Will you share it with a hungry old man who has not eaten for days?'

Dummling felt sorry for the old man. He *did* look tired and hungry. 'Of course, you are welcome to share my meal,' he said. 'But I am afraid it is not very much.'

Dummling broke the bread in half and offered the beer to the old man as they sat together on the bank in the sunshine.

Half an hour passed very happily, and Dummling discovered that the little man was full of fun. Their laughter rang through the forest, startling the birds, and making the deer pause from cropping and look at them.

Then the old man spoke. 'You have been kind to me, so I will help you. Don't cut down the tree marked with the cross, cut down that tree over there instead, and among its roots you will find something very valuable.'

With a smile and a wave, the little old man went off down the forest path. Dummling picked up his axe and walked over to the tree the old man had pointed out.

'Oh well, this one is as good as another,' he said, and swung his axe. After a few swift strokes, the blade flashing in the sunlight, the great tree came crashing to the ground, and its roots were pulled out of the earth to lie in a tangled heap on the grass. In the roots, to Dummling's open-mouthed astonishment, sat a goose with golden feathers!

Carefully and gently, he lifted the bird, stroking its feathers, and he realised they were of pure gold. This certainly was something valuable, too valuable to take home to his greedy brothers. He tucked the bird under his arm and set off for the nearest inn.

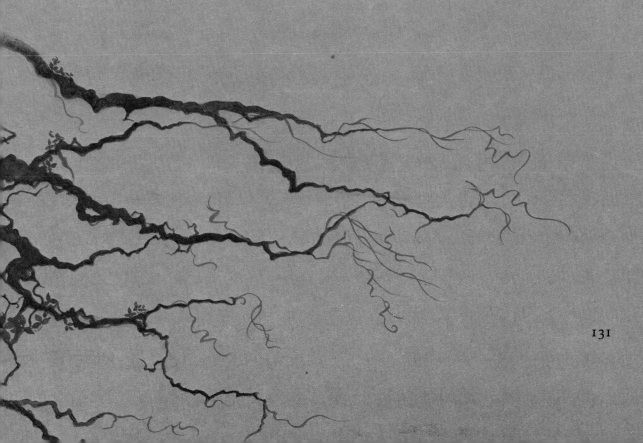

The innkeeper's daughters were full of curiosity as he showed them the goose, and told them that its feathers were golden.

'Oh, for just one of those feathers,' thought the eldest, and she planned how she might steal one.

The woodcutting and excitement had made Dummling tired, so tucking his goose gently on the end of the bed, he fell asleep. He did not hear the door creak open and the innkeeper's eldest daughter steal into the room. She was determined to have one of those lovely, golden feathers. Swiftly, she seized the goose's tail and pulled. But, imagine her surprise when she found that she could not move her hand! It was stuck fast to the goose and no matter how she tried, she could not move it.

The second daughter opened the door a crack and, like her sister, tried to snatch one of the gleaming feathers. But she, too, stuck firmly to the goose and no amount of pushing and pulling would free her.

At last the third daughter came to try her luck. But soon she joined her sisters and they all spent a very uncomfortable night in Dummling's room while he slept peacefully in his bed.

Next morning, Dummling picked up his goose without even looking, so he did not notice the three girls clinging to its feathers. He set off down the road at a brisk pace, whistling merrily and the poor girls had to run to keep up with him. When he stopped, they stopped, all bumping into each other, and when he turned right, they turned right. Wherever he went, they had

to follow. They cried out for help, and the parson, who was in his garden, hurried out to see what was the trouble. 'Shame on you!' he cried, thinking the girls were chasing Dummling, and he tried to pull them away. But he, too, was stuck fast and was soon running along behind the girls and Dummling. It was a very strange sight indeed.

As the little procession crossed the path in front of the church, the verger came running out, holding up his hands. 'Vicar, Vicar,' he cried, 'where are you going? Don't forget you have a Christening at noon.' And he took a firm grip on the parson's arm. He could not free himself, but, as he ran along behind the others, he called out to some men in a field.

'Help! Help! Do something!'

The men left their work and rushed up to the verger, but when they tried to pull him free, they, too, were stuck fast. No matter how they twisted and turned, and pulled and pushed, all seven of them were running along behind Dummling and his goose!

Without once looking back, for he was so happy, Dummling ran along the winding road, hopping and skipping and singing merrily to himself, while the luckless girls, the parson, the verger and the two farm men, hurried along behind.

At last they came to a beautiful city where the King lived in a fine castle. They could just see its battlements, with a flag flying from the topmost tower, as they hurried along. The King had a daughter of whom he was very fond, but she also made him very unhappy. She was so sad that she never, ever laughed. In desperation, the King had decreed that whoever made the Princess laugh or smile would win her hand in marriage.

At the castle gates was a large notice bearing this legend:

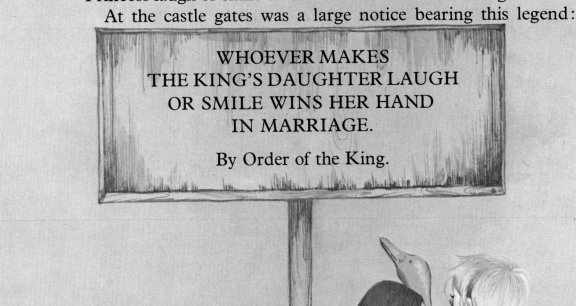

WHOEVER MAKES
THE KING'S DAUGHTER LAUGH
OR SMILE WINS HER HAND
IN MARRIAGE.

By Order of the King.

'How about that?' said Dummling to himself as he entered the city. 'So the Princess does not smile. I must see if I can cheer her up.'

The Princess was sitting by one of the castle windows as Dummling and his odd procession came through the gates. When she saw a young man, carrying a bright, golden goose under his arm and three girls, a parson, a verger and two farm workers in their smocks, trailing behind, all stuck fast, each to each, she burst out laughing. Dummling looked up and, seeing her, gave a cheery wave.

'It is a miracle,' cried the courtiers. 'The Princess is smiling, no, she is laughing! The King must be told.' And they ran to tell the King the good news.

Now the Princess was laughing so much, everyone thought she would never stop. The tears ran down her face, and all she could do was point to Dummling and his followers, and laugh and laugh and laugh.

'He is the winner,' cried the crowd, pushing Dummling forward. 'He made the Princess laugh, and he must marry her.' Everyone was laughing and cheering and waving.

Once inside the castle, the spell broke and the innkeeper's daughters, the parson, the verger and the two farm workers were all free. They all ran home before any more harm could befall them!

When the King saw Dummling he did not like the idea of letting him marry his daughter. After all, Dummling was only the son of a poor woodcutter, even if he had made the Princess happy.

So the King said that Dummling had to perform another task before he could win the Princess's hand.

'What is it?' asked Dummling.

'You must bring me someone who can drink a whole cellar full of wine,' said the King. 'That'll fix him,' he said to himself, rubbing his hands.

'I will see if I can find someone,' said Dummling and left the castle and went back to the forest. There, as he had hoped, the little old man was sitting on the tree stump.

'I have such a thirst,' the old man said, 'I could drink the sea dry, then all the rivers and all the streams.'

'Could you drink a cellar full of wine?' asked Dummling.

'A cellar full of wine!' laughed the little man, 'show me where it is. There is nothing better than wine when you are as thirsty as I am!'

So Dummling took the little old man back to the castle into the King's cellar which was brimming with wine. The casks of red and white wine were set in rows all along the walls, and Dummling did not think that anyone, especially anyone so small as his friend, could possibly drink it all.

When evening came, the old man had emptied every cask in the cellar. The King was very angry, because his trick had failed and now he had no wine left!

'All the wine is drunk,' said Dummling, 'and now I come to claim your daughter's hand in marriage.'

The King stroked his beard. He had another idea. 'There is another task to perform. Find me someone who can eat a mountain of bread.' And the King went away laughing.

Dummling returned to the tree in the forest and there, once again, he found the little, old, grey-bearded man. This time, he looked very sad and Dummling asked him what was troubling him.

'I am so hungry,' he sighed, 'that I think I could eat a mountain. I have eaten more than a hundred rolls already today, and look at my clothes, they hang on me like a sack.'

'Follow me,' said Dummling and took him back to the castle where, by the King's order, a mountain of bread was waiting. Dummling gasped at the pile of crispy, crunchy topped loaves, but the old man breathed in their smell with delight.

Hour after hour, the little man ate the bread and the mountain grew smaller and smaller until there was not one crumb left.

'The mountain of bread is eaten, not a crumb remains, so I have come to claim the Princess,' said Dummling to the King.

'Just a moment,' said the King, 'there is one more thing you have to do.' And he sat and thought and thought about it. 'Find me a ship that will sail on land as well as on water,' he said, finally. 'Then, you can marry the Princess.'

Dummling hurried back to the forest and told the little old man of the impossible task the King had set him.

'I'll never marry the Princess now,' Dummling said, and for once he was not smiling.

'Leave it to me,' said the old man. 'You helped me and, for the sake of your kind heart, I will help you again.'

So he gave Dummling a marvellous ship that could sail on land as well as water. It was a fine vessel with white, silken sails that billowed to and fro in the breeze. On the sea, the ship rose and fell like a great swan on a pond. On the land it moved just as easily, for the little old man had fitted magic wheels to propel it along the roads.

The King was delighted with his ship, for no other King, anywhere, could boast such a thing, and he was happy to give his daughter in marriage to Dummling. He had proved himself a worthy man to marry her.

The whole land rejoiced at the wedding celebrations, but Dummling insisted that the guest of honour should be the little, old, grey-bearded man who had helped him. He made him sit at the top table and made sure he was served only the finest wines and the best food.

All the people who had been stuck to the goose came too, and there was singing and dancing for hours till the castle rang with happiness.

In due time, Dummling became King and he was a very good and wise one. He never forgot the little old man of the forest, but though he often looked for him, he never found him again.

Jack and the Beanstalk

MANY, many years ago, a boy called Jack lived with his mother in a little cottage in the country. They were very poor, and often went hungry, but they did have a Guernsey cow they called Bessie. She was a fine, brown and white animal that gave more milk than any other cow in the neighbourhood. Jack was very proud of her and liked to go to market and sell butter and cheese made from her milk.

One day, his mother called him. She was looking very sad. 'It's no use, Jack,' she said, 'Bessie will have to go. I must pay the rent tomorrow and we have nothing else left to sell. Take her to the market and be sure to get as much money as you can for her.'

Sadly, Jack tied a rope to Bessie's neck and led her along the winding, dusty road to town. Usually, he enjoyed going to the town, especially on market day when the square was busy with stalls, and there were lots of people around. But today he was miserable for he liked Bessie, and he was worried about how they would manage without her.

As he walked along the road in the sunshine, Jack met an old man who asked him where he was taking the cow.

'I'm taking Bessie to market,' said Jack, 'we have no money and my mother has told me to sell her.'

'I'll buy her from you, and save you the trouble of going to market,' said the old man.

'How much will you give me?' said Jack, remembering that his mother had told him to get all the money he could for Bessie.

'I'll give you these beans in exchange for the cow,' said the old man. He opened a small bag and showed Jack the beans. Jack had never seen any beans like these before. There were five of them, all different colours, and they shone in the sunlight.

But he hesitated. What would his mother say if he came home with beans instead of money?

'These are no ordinary beans,' said the old man, 'they are *magic* beans. If you plant them, they will grow up to the sky itself!'

So Jack took the bag of beans and with a final pat, handed Bessie to the old man who led her away. Jack ran home. 'Mother,' he called, 'look what I've got!' And he showed her the bag of beans.

His mother was very angry indeed. 'You gave Bessie away for a bag of beans,' she shouted, 'you stupid boy. Now go to bed. There is no supper for you tonight.' And she wept with despair. Picking up the beans she threw them out of the window. 'What shall we do now?' she cried.

Jack fell asleep feeling very unhappy and very hungry. He woke up early the next morning feeling even more hungry. He hurried into the kitchen to look for some food and an amazing sight met his eyes!

He could see through the window a tall, green stalk climbing up and up, as far as the clouds in the sky. Great, green leaves sprouted like a ladder from top to bottom.

Jack could not wait to see where the stalk went, and, without saying goodbye to his mother, he rushed out of the cottage and started to climb. It took him a long time to reach the very top, but it was worth it. He could see for miles and the sun felt very warm on his head.

He stepped off the beanstalk on to a road that lay in front of him. It went on and on right up to the door of the biggest castle

Jack had ever seen. There was no one about, so he thought he would knock on the door and see if someone would give him some breakfast. His long climb had made him even more hungry and thirsty.

The great oak door was shut, but Jack plucked up his courage and knocked loudly. At last an old woman opened it a crack, and he asked her if she could spare some food as he had not eaten for a long time.

'Come in, come in,' she said, 'you can help with the chickens in return for a meal. But be careful of my husband. If he sees you, he will eat you up!'

She gave Jack some bread and milk, but he had only eaten half of it when he heard a very loud noise.

Bump! Thump! Bump! The walls shook and the floor moved under his feet. Jack trembled, and the milk spilled out of the bowl on to the floor.

'Quick! It's my husband,' said the old woman, 'you must hide. Into the oven with you before he sees you.'

It was dark inside the oven, but Jack peeked out of a tiny crack. A huge giant had come into the room! The giant looked all around him, and shouted,

'Fee, fi, fo, fum,
I smell the blood of an Englishman;
Be he alive or be he dead,
I'll grind his bones to make my bread.'

'Nonsense!' said his wife, 'you can smell that ox I have roasted for your breakfast. Sit down and eat it while it is hot.'

Jack had never seen anyone as big as the giant. He watched as the giant stuck his fork into huge pieces of the ox his wife had cooked for him, and the fat ran down his chin. Piece by piece, he ate a whole ox which was more food than Jack and his mother had in a year, and he washed it down with quarts of ale from a barrel at his side. At last he had had enough and he called out to his wife.

'Wife, bring me my magic hen. I want some more of her golden eggs.'

149

The giant's wife brought in a small, brown hen and put it on the table in front of her husband.

'Lay!' commanded the giant, and to Jack's astonishment, a golden egg fell on to the table. 'More!' said the giant, and soon a pile of golden eggs lay on the cloth in front of him. The giant scooped the eggs into his pocket. Then he lay back in his chair and was soon asleep. His snores were so loud that the plates on the shelf shook with the noise.

Jack crept out of the oven and, tucking the magic hen under his arm, ran as fast as his legs would carry him down the road to the beanstalk.

'Mother!' he called, 'see what I have brought!' And he put the little, brown hen on the table in the cottage and told it to lay. Soon, there was a pile of golden eggs on the table. Jack's mother could not believe her eyes as the eggs shone brightly in the light from the cottage window. She hugged Jack with joy. Now she would be able to pay the rent and buy all the food they needed. They would never be poor again.

After a while, Jack grew restless. He wanted another chance to see the giant and climb the magic beanstalk. He slipped out early, before his mother could stop him, and climbed to the top of the beanstalk. Everything was the same as before, and he lost no time in going up to the castle door. The old woman did not remember him, but she thought he would be useful to her and hid him in a cupboard when she heard the giant coming.

Thump! Bump! Thump! The walls trembled and the floor shook and the giant came into the room.

'Fee, fi, fo, fum,
I smell the blood of an Englishman,'
he bellowed, but his wife cut him short.

'Rubbish! You have such a cold you cannot smell anything,' she snapped. 'Now do stop all that noise and eat this sheep I've roasted for you.'

Now the only sound that Jack could hear was the giant eating, and piece by piece a whole sheep disappeared down his great throat. Jack was amazed!

When he had finished eating, the giant called out to his wife.

'Wife, bring me the key to my treasure chest.'

The giant's wife brought in an enormous iron key and the
giant opened the huge chest standing by the table. It was
piled high with bags full of golden coins! Jack watched as the
giant counted the coins out into two big sacks.

After such a huge meal, the giant found all this counting very
tiring, and he began yawning, and soon lay back in his chair fast
asleep. His great snores sounded like thunder. Jack crept from his
hiding place and, snatching one of the sacks, ran along the road
and slid down the beanstalk.

'Mother! Mother!' he shouted, 'look what I have brought you this time!'

His mother scolded him a little, but she was delighted with the coins. She had never seen so many, and they gave up trying to count them all.

'No more visits to the giant,' she warned Jack, but he only laughed. He wanted to go once more to the giant's castle.

So, next morning, he got up early and climbed to the top of the beanstalk and hurried along the path to the castle. Jack was afraid that the old woman might not let him in again so he crept in through a window and hid behind a huge milk churn.

The walls shook and the floor trembled and Jack knew the giant was coming!

> *'Fee, fi, fo, fum,*
> *I smell the blood of an Englishman.*
> *Be he alive or be he dead,*
> *I'll grind his bones to make my bread.'*

The giant's voice echoed around the room and Jack began to wish that he had listened to his mother and not climbed the beanstalk again. The giant looked in the oven, then he looked in the cupboard, but just as he was getting close to Jack's hiding place, the old woman bustled in.

'What are you doing?' she said crossly. 'Come and eat your breakfast.' So the giant sat down to his breakfast of five roast hens and ten loaves of bread.

When the giant had finished eating, Jack wondered what he would do. After all, he no longer had so much money, or his golden egg laying hen! Jack didn't have long to wait.

'Wife!' shouted the giant, 'open my box of jewels!' The giant's wife opened the huge box and as Jack watched, the giant thrust his hand inside it and took out red rubies that were as dark as blood, sapphires as blue as the sky and diamonds as big as hens' eggs. But the giant soon tired of looking at the jewels, and leaving the box open by his chair, he ordered his wife to bring his harp.

This was the most beautiful harp Jack had ever seen, for it was made of pure and shining gold that sparkled and shimmered as the giant gently plucked the strings. The giant told the harp to play him a lullaby. The soft, sweet music flowed into the room, and soon its gentle sounds were replaced by the giant's snores. He was fast asleep.

Jack crept out once more from his hiding place and snatched some of the jewels. Then he looked at the harp. It was too beautiful to leave behind so he picked it up. But as he touched it, the harp began to call out, 'Master! Master!' The strings twanged and twisted and woke the giant with their noise.

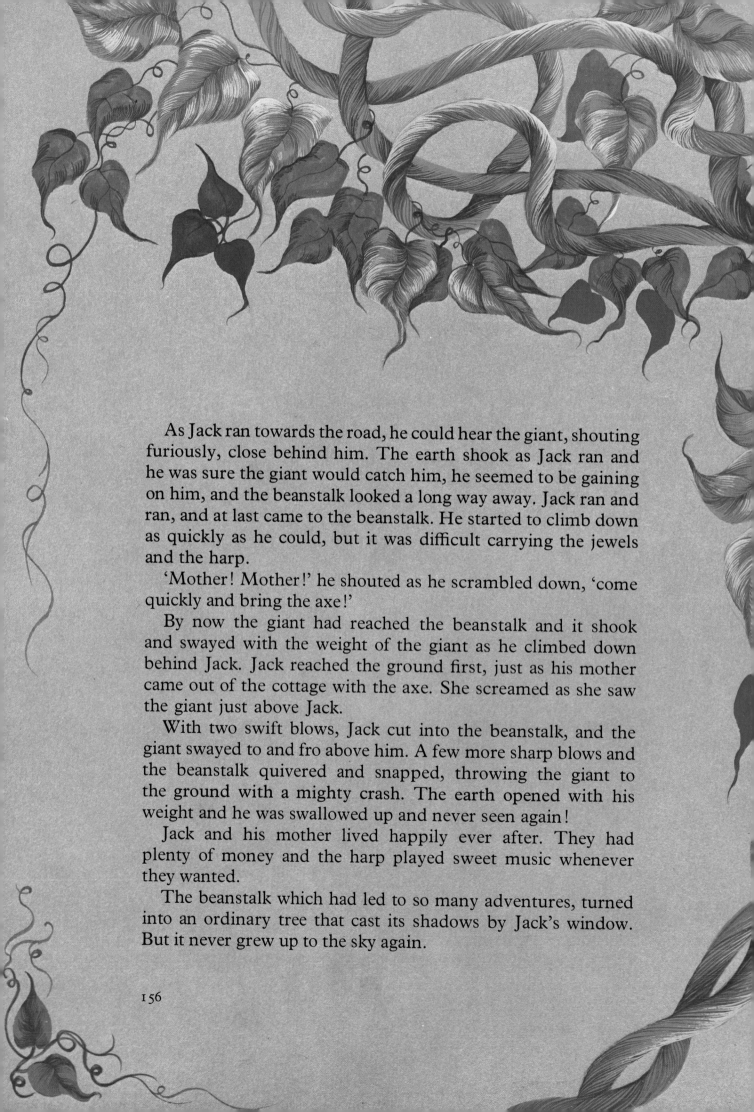

As Jack ran towards the road, he could hear the giant, shouting furiously, close behind him. The earth shook as Jack ran and he was sure the giant would catch him, he seemed to be gaining on him, and the beanstalk looked a long way away. Jack ran and ran, and at last came to the beanstalk. He started to climb down as quickly as he could, but it was difficult carrying the jewels and the harp.

'Mother! Mother!' he shouted as he scrambled down, 'come quickly and bring the axe!'

By now the giant had reached the beanstalk and it shook and swayed with the weight of the giant as he climbed down behind Jack. Jack reached the ground first, just as his mother came out of the cottage with the axe. She screamed as she saw the giant just above Jack.

With two swift blows, Jack cut into the beanstalk, and the giant swayed to and fro above him. A few more sharp blows and the beanstalk quivered and snapped, throwing the giant to the ground with a mighty crash. The earth opened with his weight and he was swallowed up and never seen again!

Jack and his mother lived happily ever after. They had plenty of money and the harp played sweet music whenever they wanted.

The beanstalk which had led to so many adventures, turned into an ordinary tree that cast its shadows by Jack's window. But it never grew up to the sky again.

157